THOUGHTS ON THE WIND

SELECTED POEMS

by John Gilbert Fuller

Copyright © 2016 by John Gilbert Fuller

Published by Woodbridge Publishing Company
Haworth, NJ 07641

All Rights Reserved
First Edition

ISBN 978-1-890597-02-3

Library of Congress Control Number: 2016905529

Printed in the United States of America

Contents

Seed 1
Symphony 6
Play 11
Vantage 15
Pull 27
Veil 34
Road and Return 46
Release 53
Treasure 61
Departure 67
Knot 70
Mist 72
Connection 80
Construct 88
Seasons 92
Cantigny 94
Art 109

Index *113*

Seed

THOUGHT PASSAGE VITAL FORCE

I wait upon the vital force,
Core of creation's art,
For molding essence on the page
With unknown end at start.

A word, a phrase, formed to engage,
Day's *wind thought* mood to find,
With mental intrigue shaping quest,
Sense metered rhyme to bind.

And when it's done there's still no rest
Though source has flown away.
Interpretation may be wrong:
Translation's false word play.

So ever must formed sensate song
Be scored without remorse
To sharpen, hone which may prolong
Felt passage vital force.

And if result at last seems true
Time space re-echoes ever new.
8-24-06

IN TIME SPACE WEND ALONG

Of rivers, forests, meadows, sky
Of lake-sea and its coast
Of ocean vistas stretching grand
Blend mixtures matter most,
Impressing sight with beauty's stand,
Bold colors painting light
With season's added awesome spice
For passage soul's delight.

Found growth change vibrance does entice
With magnet's echo song
Expanding self's emotions fed
In time space wend along.

Each beauty spot where thoughts were bred
Entwines its mystery sigh,
A part of me where'er I'm led
To live beneath the sky.
7-26-06

AND WOULD YOU LEAD ANOTHER LIFE?

And would you lead another life?
The devil you don't know?
What are conditions you would name
To orchestrate *your* show
If you had god force to proclaim,
When doomed with life to live,
But then allowed the *time,* the *place,*
Race, prowess, friends to sieve?

What *gender* choose to run life's race?
Untested times or past?
How shape charisma on earth's tract?
Would *health* be first or last?
Would *wealth, luck, happiness* fill pact?
Would *beauty* conquer *strife*?
Would world's *pain* be a sterling fact?
Would *fame* grace imposed life?

And if reprieved by force on high
Would then you breathe eternal sigh?
6-24-04

ANGEL HAIRED GODDESS

The weed pods here along lake shore
Show cotton flares of white
With wind gusts pulling seeds to fly,
Sail swirls adrift in flight.

And as white slew comes whipping by
One lands to cling on me,
Brown seed attached to angel hair
Full essence now to see.

Held by brown seed, threads stream on air,
Blown wondrous in strong breeze,
Like Goddess silver hair blown long,
Head image shape to please.

And when released she's airborne song,
Grace streaming off before,
A silvan Goddess midst white throng
On journey by lake shore!

What more of tale is there to tell
As Goddess image thought does dwell!
10-25-11

TWO POPLAR SEEDS

Two poplar seeds drift-float lake air
In time-space for year's flow.
But weather's odd chill force it seems
Delays time's white glut show.

Yet lonely seeds still carry dreams
Of future poplar stand
And though delayed air's wandering two
Grip white sail hope schemes grand.

While lacking spurts of crowded spew
They paint drift-beauty sight,
Creating thought-desires of sea
Where pagan lures delight!

Yet lustful thoughts here cannot free
Soul from aged body care
Though youth-felt passions never flee
It's mind's flight world they share!

6-07-13

Symphony

DAY'S SONG

The breeze and I up on lake's hill,
Beneath oak's leafy sway,
Will meld in morning's hour here
Midst lake view's grand display.

Blue sky above holds half moon sphere
That smiles upon the scene
Where rain storms came then passed on by
Yet gave lawns freshened green.

A finch, a jet, flit butterfly,
High, low, and in between,
Are parallel in lines of flight
With passage through lake scene!

Time spent with breeze's kiss delight
Beneath grand oak on hill,
With lake's view spread before my sight,
Has never failed to thrill.

And while I know I'll soon be gone
Its echo memory sings day's song!
8-07-12

MORNING SHADOWS CREEP

There are geese that float on forest lake
But most fly crisscross by
Seen wanderlings
Sunned morning brings
With trailing *squawks* on high.

But morning's light has shadow wings
From cloud creep on sky's blue
Returning chill
Night's depth did spill
Till morning sunlight grew.

And when I came sun's flooding thrill
Had warmed the air around
Glow shining leaves
On forest trees
Hued symphony profound.

But now shade shadows, chilling breeze,
Send warmth upon its way
As geese awake
On forest lake
Cruise *squawking* rage on day.
10-27-05

BIRD CHORUS MORNING

So many mixed bird voices here,
Note repetitions heard,
In sunshine morning by the shore.
Not love songs from each bird!

And yet delightful, chorus score,
That orchestrates the day,
Where lake is calm though hushing breeze
Marks gentle surface sway.

While many darting bird shapes tease,
Finch gallops midst flights seen.
His yellow streak line threads the air
To contrast mowed slope green.

It is day's morning gift I share
As cardinal, red, skims near.
And crescent moon in blue sky fair
Adds spice to atmosphere!

Lake view embraces all around
As morning swells each bird scale sound!
5-14-12

A LITTLE WHILE

A little while, a little while
Of peace to contemplate
The floating gray-white carpet mist
Sun rays evaporate.

Low early morning sky is kissed
With orange ball of sun
In lift flare from horizon's line
Dissolving cloud damp spun.

The passage starry night design
Of dense dark into haze
Which cloud tinge orange filters blue
Holds fresh white morning's glaze.

There are no others near to view
The morning's peaceful style
As field mist blanket thins thick spew
To contemplate awhile.
8-07-06

SKY'S OCEAN SHORE

Dense cover cloud upon the sky
—Land continent to see—
Has long shore edging water's blue
With ocean stretching free.

There are two islands, small, in view,
Just off the cloud's lined shore,
White puffs of vapor slow to move
In sky's theme etched before.

Blue ocean's stretch has channel groove
—Like seen on many maps—
As now the islands, creep-drift change,
Fuse on sky pictured gaps!

Sky's vapor islands rearrange
Design up in cloud sky
—Thin, disappearing wisping range—
That joins cloud shore on high.

Sky's land-meld-ocean drifts along
Distinct blue-white evolving song!
5-29-12

Play

CONSIDER

Consider a tree in the spring
Consider a stretch of the beach
Consider, consider, my mind's all a dither
Consider an apple or peach.

Consider that cloud in the sky
Consider that girl and that boy
Consider, consider, the world's all a quiver
Consider love's wondrous joy.

Consider the moon's lack of heat
Consider some ice cream and pie
Consider, consider, how snakes always slither
Consider the eye of a fly.

Consider the sun's burning rays
Consider the cat down the street
Consider, consider, go thither, come hither
Consider your marvelous feet.

Consider a horse when it neighs
Consider how women drink stout
Consider, consider, there's no meaning to 'prither'
Consider the effort to shout.

Consider the litter about
Consider the robin that sings
Consider, consider, how values do wither
Consider impractical things!
4-22-1982

SANDPIPER

Sandpiper, sandpiper, hopping so near
Sandpiper, sandpiper, bring me good cheer
The sun's at its zenith
The water is clear
Sandpiper, sandpiper, bring me my dear.

Dear one, oh dear one, come sit by my side
Dear one, or dear one, your face do not hide
The breezes are blowing
Our ship's on the tide
Dear one, oh dear one, life's crest we must ride.

Kiss me my darling while sun's in the sky
Each day moves to ending, each love too soon dies
Kiss me my darling, forget all earth's ties
Brave our sweet madness, love's season is nigh.

9-12-67

SAND PIPER BY LAGOON

Sand Piper! Sand Piper!
Why are you here
Beneath the Hawthorne tree?

Beside lagoon
Where robins croon
And not beside sand sea?

I came to hear the bells strike noon
And saw you pecking round
As leg stems race
Peck other place
From tree shade to lawn ground.

And though the martins swoop your grace,
As robins come and go,
You circle grass
Near my bench pass
With skitters fast and slow.

Sand Piper! Sand Piper! Lad or lass?
Where can your soul mate be?
Proud markings clear
While racing near
But why not by lake-sea?

6-20-05

BLUE DRAGONFLY

Lone dragonfly puts on a show
Of speed and derring-do
Out in the sun
Full stop then run
Reversing zone he flew

Blue body glints out in the sun
He skirts tree shadows by
With short sorties
Dive lifts in breeze
Bold dashes low nearby

I wonder at raced oval tease
Above lawn's shaded green
With drift edge touch
Shade depth too much?
Felt peril 'neath its screen?

And still it dashes, tree bound clutch
Invades shade, hovers there
Now out in glow
Wings, brake-speed, slow
Then surge darts round through air

6-14-01

Vantage

CAMELOT'S DREAM

Upon the iridescent sky I gazed
Amazed by blues and whites of varied shade
The clouds a gauze of pictures on parade
Enhanced by jet trail etching line that mazed
With intricate blue highlights coming through.

Then I lowered my gaze unto the land,
A landscape of lagoon by sculpted hills
Fresh grasses green to trees majestic thrills
With pathway winding round a fairyland,
Another world which I was blessed to view.

Camelot's dream the landscape there did paint
While silent, high, a jet laced sky so quaint.
5-05-94

WONDER'S SPELL

How many times in wonder's spell
Is glow reflected on?

I know from youth such moments spent
Were never dwelt upon
And but relived, when mind search went,
To write it all again!

And such, recalled, has faded feel
Till page renews youth's glen
But here today reflection's wheel
Knows wondrous day's caress.

Not racing through each moment found
Yet lost soon none the less.

For moments lived through sense compound
Have but one place to dwell;
And then they move to mind built ground
That changes what befell!

Yet youth felt wonder page evokes
Still limns fade shadows time provokes
8-14-01

RIVER BEND'S AUTUMN SCENE

Far sunlit autumn river scene,
Past leaf drift water flow,
At bend above the waterfall,
Has color depth bright show.

Bank's red shrub leaves like dense hedge wall
Glows 'neath trees orange stand,
Reflecting echoed water hues
Onto bend's river strand.

It contrasts with grove's near bank views,
Leaf sky streaks flooding air,
From twisted dried brown shedding trees,
In front of others bare.

It almost seems the morning breeze
That whispers in between,
Denuding bank and leaf bright frieze,
Embalms far autumn scene!
10-23-06

LAKE-SEA'S UNSEEN FACE

Wild is the lake shore's raging sea
Crest waves foamed white on brown
That roil beach sand,
Stained width stretch band
Out to expanse renown
Where brown goes green into blue's stand
Of depth miles out from shore,
Unseen today
Where rage waves play
In curved scoop coast before.

Yet, if on high, the lake-sea's way
Would show itself as blue
Throughout expanse
Which coasts enhance
With pale edged washing spew.
But on this beach where crests entrance
With roaring foam white waves
There's not a trace
Of sea's blue face
That sky's view-sight engraves!
4-13-05

PERFECTION STRIVING

Why does the thought expressed back then
Need changing here today?
Like craftsman I am haunted by
Work finished...but must lay
Mind thought upon words gleaming ply
To polish-tweak it more.

Yet when I did new sense was wrought
From what glowed there before!
Was sense right then?
While now has caught,
With one word switched around,
A different meaning depth compare!

But is it more profound!?
Or has changed sense destroyed what's fair,
Which time revealed pure then?
And word replacement-tweak from air
Might need be changed again!

Perfection striving has its cost
Once gained, but changed, it could be lost!
Perfection glimmer's road along:
Perceived attainment — Siren's song!

9-17-07

PERSPECTIVE TRUTH

I wonder if the truth I've found
Is really truth at all?
No matter what old teachers said
New facts learned can appall!

And science probing some new thread
Reverses what time's grown,
Instilled by school when I was young,
With new facts then unknown.

Yet once reversals are begun,
—Old facts tarred black made white
—What comes when future minds amend
Our world to set things right?

And as our cosmos ethers wend,
Infusing change profound,
Is truth a fluid mixture blend
For each age to compound?

In biased love-hate world I see
Whose slave to truth can set one free?
8-08-12

AND DO I REALLY CARE?

I wonder if I really care
In wander life along
When reading each day's hateful news,
Proud leaders strewing wrong?

The centuries hate as Arab views
Israeli nation's stand
To justify with righteousness
Their terrorists at hand?

America's aggressiveness
Proclaimed in freedom's name
Pre-emptive war with spreading blight
For reason that proved lame?

Where's gone peace, love, forgiving might,
Power tolerance to share?
Must faith bred evil always fight!
And do I really care?

7-28-06

1890'S HISTORIC FARM CONTRAST

Dress contrast marks the simpler life
In hot day's summer air
With farmer women dresses long
Beneath straw bonnets flare.

With garden rakes, from sleeved arms strong,
They scrape earth in boots black;
Their aproned fronts, high collars tight,
Have but flow dress length slack!

Apposed to gingham clothes hued bright
The tourists here to see
Have bared limbs and soft sneakered feet
Cloth cover sparse and free.

It speaks, I think, to freedom's beat
Across years crowding life;
And while the simpler times bore heat
Stressed moderns would ease strife!
6-05-06

FRESH PERSPECTIVES

I took a page from yesterday
And found fresh place to be
Where all's familiar and yet strange
In garden's world to see.

It gives perspective deeper range
To find familiar new
To see what wasn't found before
In static parts of view.

Much like those times upon the shore,
Lake-sea, the sky, lap waves!
Familiar place in time that's gone
Which memory still engraves.

And midst here's garden color song
Time's lure where memories play
Is yet a place where I belong
Like lake-sea off away.

These beauty places that I've known
Are magnets for ideas sown!
7-10-13

ZEN GARDEN (*KARE-SAN-SUI*)

Dry-mountain-water garden sphere
On island with Scotch pines
Whose flat limbs out,
Bonsai'd grace shout,
Near stone raked ripple lines,
Is really not a place of drought
On island water scene
Of eastern grace
Wend pathways trace
Through pines and yews deep green.

And with the fall red-yellows race
Past ornate lanterned stone
Quaint tea house stead
Shrub green lines thread
To paint dry-water zone.

Illusion marks Zen's garden bed
In lake-lagoon surround.
Three islands here
Far eastern sphere
That feels like sacred ground.
10-25-04

VAN GOGH'S ASTOUND

What gives some artists broad command
And lays world at their feet?
Then fades away,
Past living day,
Ignored when life's complete?

And what gives art immortal sway?
Appreciated then
However found
Van Gogh's astound?
Obscured in life span when
The artist toiled in sacred ground
Brave outlook for the world!
Defined new ways
Enlightened phase
With pathways far unfurled?

What is art's penetrating gaze?
Beyond creator's mind
That meets demand
Let's it expand
Revered as classic find?

And what force girds luck's rousing fame
That lacks of art's enduring flame?

7-15-01

SONOMA'S PORTUGUESE BEACH WITH GULL

The ocean breeze up on cliff shore
Bites through day's sun flood might
As waves below
Crash foam wash show:
Spilled shaving cream rush sight!

And round rock isles waves also glow
Accenting upthrusts dark
White raging flares
Split roll surge glares
To match beach foam's rush stark.

Where bay beach paints the white it wears
There's contrast of washed land:
Gray hued sand beach;
Brown hills bare reach;
And green-red gorse cliff spanned.

A friendly gull glides down with screech
Wing grace descent from air
Pink legs before
Cliff edge his floor
Wind ruffled feathers flair.

An ocean idyll stretches here
With artful gull on guard march near.

9-28-01

Pull

THE WAYWARD HEART

My soul would go a-journeying
Beyond the rock bound sea
My heart would stay a-lingering
To feel itself in thee.

Two forces that are counter bound
Make war with indecision
Two principals and both profound
Have clouded o'er my vision.

Your refuge and your loving touch
Can wake in me such joy
When you are here my space is such
No other thought can buoy.

Yet when you're gone my soul does cry
For paths left there to roam
While mystery in all I spy
Keeps calling me back home.

I'm just a pawn exposed to light
Twice captured on this battle site.

8-04-94
Best Poets of 2014 Submission 5/12/14
Eber & Wein Publishers

DAYS OF SUMMER WANDER ON

The days of summer wander on
So different from before
When morning, afternoon or night
Held wonders by the shore.

But even so thought days in flight
Have nurtured me along
With other lures from earth's expanse
To sing poetic song.

Now other vistas must enhance
Must stimulate the mind
Give purpose to each summer day
Worked energies refined.

For without such along the way
With depth power essence drawn
Upon some page with artful play
I could not greet the dawn!
8-11-06

SOUL'S WORTH GOAL

Thought trails compound is found outside
In nature's garden world
Where days of Summer, Spring and Fall
Paint varied scenes unfurled!

The weather, mostly, dictates all
The action thoughts I find
To weave in beauty's patterned scroll
Those words that then unwind!

Life's purpose, found, imbued this role,
Those many years ago,
When I sought freedom from life's chains
That would not let me grow.

For parents, schooling, social gains,
Imposed life's time-space mold
To strengthen and perpetuate
Loved people in its fold!

And while *here's* wonders educate
And gild life on its tide,
If one could let such goals placate,
My soul could not abide!

And chose far different way to go
Which gleans soul's worth from *wind thought* flow!
6-03-11

MOTHER NATURE'S MORNING TEASE

Gazebo's padded chair today,
Pond fountain's jet spray white,
Is place and view with cool breeze shade
In morning's wending flight.

For sun beats fierce with heat's parade
This depth of Summer morn.
And I need breeze's cool caress
For work's thought to be born.

Now suddenly surprise does bless
My thoughts, this place, and me,
As turkey mother with chicks pass,
Day's pond-walk oddity!

Wild turkeys here as flock can mass
Cantigny meadow's way.
But here lone mother with kid class
Makes pond walk stroll today!?

Mother Nature's my constant tease
Creating image thoughts to please!
7-16-13

FISH SPLASH LURE

Brisk breeze refreshes atmosphere,
Of morning's rising heat,
Beside small lake in pine grove shade
Beyond sun's glaring beat!

Across the way a picnic's laid
Beneath large umbra tree,
Out of the sun, awaiting noon,
With anguished child to see.

His mother calms him. *It's too soon!'*
As brother fly casts bait.
Yet he is anxious, leaving pole,
As if he too can't wait!

Then fish leap *'splat'* reclaims his soul.
Both lads dash focused cheer,
Encouraged by large fish seen whole
That charges atmosphere!

The fish leap seen has brought lads joy
As both now casting rods employ.
No longer seem the lads to care
About the picnic table fare!
6-11-12

HUGE BOULDER ROCK

Not often do I come just here
To open field lake hill.
But sun is blocked by slate cloud sky,
Breeze fresh with sweeping thrill.

And on this field huge rock looms by,
An artifact with grace.
The green lush lawn's proud ornament
Of lake field picnic place.

Huge boulder rock seems permanent,
Small mesa style cliff side,
A lure to me each time I passed
To come and sit beside.

The muted sun and brisk breeze cast
Propelled my steps to veer
From oak tree's shaded lake view vast
For grass field's atmosphere!

And here the morning feels just right
As cotton seeds swoop, soar air flight!
6-21-13

ANCIENT CHINESE WILDERNESS POETRY

The clarity, the dark,
The ancient and the new.
An age old link now felt between
For mind thoughts to pursue!

Translation's language blocks
—Removed by toiler's ken—
East's pictographic arcane art
Restoring wisdom's fen.

There were not airplaned skies!
Worlds found, Kingfisher green,
Where mind felt essence rivers flow
With spirits honed and keen.

Now link returns to bind
Old essence, rebirth sigh,
As common spirit mountain peaks
Fling wisdom from the sky!
4-03-07

Veil

MIND VIEW FORCE

We think we see what others see
And yet we never do!
And what I mean by that is this
From samples wandered through:

The world of heartache from love's kiss
While her heart coolness churns;
Snow's silent beauty scene before
While neighbor warm clime yearns!

The ocean's crashing storm waves roar
Is awesome show or sailor's blight;
The heavens winking stars above
Are mysteries sought or just night's light.

And though each holds reactive love
That others do not see
We look and think we know whereof
Mind view force ought to be!
12-30-05

WHAT, INTO THE NIGHTINGALE'S SONG

What, into the nightingale's song,
Forgets the mind to hear?
What, when gazing from Ossa's peak,
Becomes the next frontier?

When voice does shout but words don't speak
Where finds the soul its guide?
And on the shore with waves and breeze
Where does awe's wonder hide?

When rippling stream cannot appease
The pain your heart does bear
Where bides new love as echoes wing
A perfume to compare?

For all the journeys left may bring
Bold hints that don't belong
When dark a shadow there does sting
Its flight from past so strong.

8-01-95
First published in American Poetry Annual 1997 by the Amherst Society
commemorating Emily Dickinson.

IN THE WOODS WITH FAR DESIRE

In the woods with far desire
I hear a haunting song:
Lonesome bird trill does conspire
At scenes that don't belong
Among the shadows damp despair
Among the rocks and leaves
Among down branches once blown fair
Among displacement trees.

The notes swell odd into the sky
Into the air that blows
Gone sorrow mixed with happy cry
Of land sweet water knows.

I muse on notes and wonder why
Such song does touch my heart
Impelling wish from lips to fly
Yet leaves me here apart.

And then mind wakes to conscious themes
The robin on the path
The wayward sense of all my dreams
The world in aftermath.

4-12-96
Published in Best Poets and Poems of 2012 by World Poetry Movement

WHAT EYES ALLOW

Ego must shrink to reach the goal
Of truth residing there
Amongst the folds
That time withholds
Back when the world seemed fair.

The mystery your mind enfolds
Cloaked like remembered dream
Defeats the plan
Of truth to scan
When self rules all supreme.

But when replayed without the man
You hold yourself to be
Observing now
What eyes allow
Relationships to see
You'll feel what she had felt somehow
Across the wastes of time
And light will stroll
Events seen whole
As truth from dark does climb.
2-07-97

SOUND MYSTERIES SOUGHT

I seek effect of foreign sounds,
Of words mind can not hear,
Those sense-filled Chinese singing tones
For pictograph art's ear.

As poetry, for me, evokes
Itself in tone played chimes,
Heard ghosts impressed through metered voice
Lilt sense felt echoed rhymes.

And though translation often gives
A view of thoughts that were,
Old sounding echo-accents flown
New minds can but infer!

And I regret lost art-filled sound,
Though sense has been transferred,
Creation's transposed image seen
But no sound echoes heard.

Perhaps, in far met other world,
Word echoes sown will sound unfurled.
4-10-07

RED MAPLE LEAVES

Upon park bench in shaded place
The heat is rising fast
With Summer warmth of glory felt
That spites wet season's past.

I'm early here so I won't melt
With sun's force high in sky.
And yet on ground and bench beside
Red maple leaves are by.

Like yesterday there is a tide
Of leaf gusts on the air.
Fall's red despite tree's shading green
This Summer day must share.

Displacement days are often seen,
In years of life span grace,
Yet still remarkable bench scene
In this loved beauty place.

For world's aren't often what they seem
In season's passage or night's dream!
9-10-13

THE BOOKS ARE TOO MANY

The books are too many, the days too few
To read them all and find if aught's been missed
Which should have been granted my heart's assist,
Adding such to my small list for review
When soul craves fond companion to enjoy.

Down the years my list has quietly grown
But mostly from ages past have friends come,
New found delight midst modern tedium
Flooding our shelves with tripe that's overblown
But sates demand for publishers employ.

So many the books I've read for the nonce
Swallowed by Lethean water's response.
1-6-94

DREAM FANTASY

Dream fantasy still haunts the day
That's chill with Autumn's touch
While body's sense holds youthful glow
Denied by age as such.

But like here's Summer-Autumn show
The sense-feel love dream cast
Is time's felt unreality
Of mind-world passions past.

Impotent wish-reach fantasy
That body can't attain
Etch painted on mind's fertile screen
To ease day's present pain.

And like lake's ending Summer scene
With Fall's chill marring day
Mind's fantasy of youth so keen
Is time's warp gone astray.

And yet mind images that tease
Reflect how youthful strength could please!
9-17-13

WHAT IS TRUE KNOWLEDGE?

What is true knowledge? What's to know
Beyond our daily ken?
How many seekers seek behind
For depths of time-space when
Narrators wrote creed words that bind
To learn how minds were skewed?
To learn how filter-shades of light
Held shadowed dark imbued
As truth's voice sounding took its flight
With error's shade in place
To shape young future minds in mold
With man forged errant grace?

But there are proofs yet to behold
Refining what we know
To pale the shadowed light in gold
And ride truth's river flow!
2-20-06

DISTORTION'S GAZE

We often think that truth is known
From witnesses who see
And than report, at later time,
The facts as they must be!

And science, too, with lens sublime
Explores our finite world
Presenting facts from what's been found
Proclaiming truth unfurled.

Yet with results mind's fault is bound,
Perspective's mold that views,
Distortion bent which contemplates
Found facts in mythic hues!

Perhaps one day confusing fates
Will let pure truth be known
With non-distortion that relates
What patent facts have shown.

But yet until such fateful day
Distorted mind sight shows the way!
5-05-05

WHEN ROME ROARED AS A CHILD OF POWER

When Rome roared as a child of power
And Greece's glory glowed entire
There came on man one fateful hour
To cast aside his base desire
And choose a path that held a key
To spiritual doors of ecstasy

Then with new banner raised on high
And burning breasts of righteousness
The key was cast into the mire
While molding Rome to blessedness
The hour was gone, the key debased
As man his love of war embraced

1-28-70

THE BARK

Carried through deepening veils of night
O'er ghostly waters slow ebbing tide
Seeking, oh seeking, each glimmer for light
As echoes come calling, calling, to chide
Of the thirst and the hope implanted by dreams
Adrift in a bark where no compass gleams.

Go back, go back, but where can land be
To grip and to taste and to hold 'til the dawn.
Echoes in darkness resound of the sea!
Through mist and through fog our shadow has gone
As gently, so gently, the tide creates flight
Rushing through deepening veils of night.

1-13-70

Road and Return

CHANGE AND RECALL

This place today of lake shore view
Has changed since last year here.
Shade trees now droop with denser leaves
And widened shadow sphere.

Yet birds still nestle midst the trees
Chirp, song notes on the air
As sea gull swoops along the shore,
White wings low passing flair!

Yet somehow vista spread before
Seems different here today
As drooping leaves design on sky
Has realigned lake's bay.

But yet lake ripples drifting by
Breeze patterned surface view
Where fishermen cast arch lines high
Lets past invade what's new!

And, now recalled, here was first place
I ever came to view lake's grace!
7-11-13

KLINE CREEK FARM SCENE

The creek flows rapid, wending way,
Through 'Living History Farm,'
Its banks dredge-etched from washing rains,
Clear stream-rush shade-light charm.

A goose on islet near complains
At me, admiring scene,
While leaning wood rail over stream
Of creek's shade dappling green.

Farm bridge lane passageway limns dream
Of history's living past:
In 1890's farm world place
There's horse manure cast.

Along dirt lane, straw-droppings trace
—From field's plow work of day
—And lead to red barn's farmyard grace
Where farmer makes his way.

And now farm bell by kitchen rings
As 1890's time frame sings!
5-07-07

LONE GULL HOME

First sight in lake view morning sky
Is herring gull's white wings
Grace circling flight
Of pure delight
With echoes lake-sea sings.

But since lone gull is frequent sight
Here's space must now be home
Away from sea
Where he should be
Enjoying wave spray foam.

Perhaps from storm-rage gull did flee,
Lost in wind currents blast,
To find, rage gone,
Lake's inland dawn
Where fate his lot has cast.

Now soaring lake shore on and on,
—Seen often when I'm here—
Arch gull wings ply
Past herons by
Through found world's atmosphere.
7-16-08

COME! WALK WITH ME

Come! Walk with me in the garden while
The butterfly there wings
Consent to stroll once more with me
Amongst bright colored things
Remember back when we were free
To love as hearts entwined
Remember all the foolish times
We romped to others blind
Inciting jealous rage betimes
Ignoring hearts that cared
Then flown like smoke when war did blast
Our fleeting sighs despaired
So walk with me as in the past
Old war cannot beguile
Think not of ages long since passed
And walk with me awhile

8-10-95

THE OTHER SIDE OF YESTERDAY

The other side of yesterday
Beyond the years flown by:
Son's death-pain sea,
New goal for me:
To find worth 'neath earth's sky.

Law's unknown pelf? or simple tree?
That stands in forest's way,
With peace there bred
In nature's stead
Midst joyous bird song play?

Could all life's worries then be fled?
Would children's lives be flayed?
Was death the sign
For fate's design
With future treasures laid?

How would itself torn soul align?
What star on high to guide
Along the way
Each passing day
Until life found worth's bride?

Through claiming years there's been a song
With unseen touch of hand along
To fend disasters through bad days
And still is felt in many ways!

7-18-13

LAKE-SEA AND OCEAN'S GRACE

Utterly different the vast lake-sea
Than ocean's foam spilled way
Where island rocks
Jut granite shocks
In far Sonoma bay

And larger gulls make up their flocks
Of varied color lines
But just as tame
Play wind soar's game
Where sunset coast defines.

So other seen and yet the same
Vast waters stretching out
With sea and sky
In endless ply
Beyond mind echo's shout

For seas flow endless to the eye
With waters calming sound
Though both may be
When raging free
Storm monsters force compound

Yet more of life has found me here
Where vast lake-sea impresses cheer
10-03-01

1890 FARM'S APPEAL

It is a door to long gone world
When walking farm lane way.

At creek's board bridge you enter in
Old time-sense feel display.
Vibration, people, round you spin
With aura's seen as real.

You are a ghost from forward age
That's fled its gloss appeal.
Technologies that rule this stage
Are horse drawn carts and men,
With ladies milking, toting grain
From meadow past pig pen.

As ghost you shuffle off life's strain,
From speeding car-stressed world,
As anvil *clangs* workshop again,
Farm's peaceful scene unfurled.
Though toil was hard and life was rough
For day's found moment it's enough!

Nostalgia over, you return
To world gone farmers once did yearn.
9-13-07

Release

MEASURED TIME

Our bodies travel measured time
Mind lodged in living cells
Which age and die and recreate
Fleshed homes where mind-self dwells.

Yet time the body will defeat
Its elements reclaim
As food or soil or cosmic air
Recycling star world's game.

But mind in flight goes anywhere
Within time's measured scale:
The past, the future, cosmic space
While locked in earthly jail!

Mind-prison questions ever race
Through life of measured time:
'Are there dimensions past time-space
For freed self force sublime?'
7-20-06

BROWN OAK LEAF CLING

The little oak tree in depth snow
Against white Winter view
Of Silver Lake and far tree stand
Flits cling-leaves brown in hue.

Against snow's white and dark tree stand
Brown's contrast is delight
Just like lake-surface fishers there
With colored jackets, sleds, in sight.

A cheerful Winter scene to share
Accented by small tree
That seems to shiver in chill breeze
Through trembling leaves flit-spree.

Dried brown is burnished memory tease
Midst sunlit lake view show
In morning with blue sky to please
And drift puff clouds like snow!

1-28-11

WHEN INTO DARKNESS

When into darkness I wander alone
Untethered from symbols imposing might
It's from within that I must find the light.
Not my own but that which at birth was sown,
It's source hidden, yet there, remarking me.
It's part of me but it's alien too.

More like a passageway lit from above
Harsh clarity not often warmed by love.
Yet it can guide when dark does renew
Not mindful that it still glows midst debris.
When light returns to its source in the end
Will it be *me* who's there to ascend?

10-7-94

THE SEA GULLS

From off the bending mast the sea gulls fly,
Their flapping wings retreat against the sky.
Oh, would that I from out this leadened coil
Could seek in freedom flight from mortal toil
These rising birds on wing in fading light.

Across my cheeks the spray so wetly stings
As coming 'bout the clapping sail taut springs.
Arched way in foaming white the sharp bow cleaves
Through racing waters, homeward turned, and leaves
A squawked, gull echo, sounding on the night.

9-4-1958
Published in Poetry Today Fall Quarterly 2006
Publication of International Society of Poets

PILLARS OF THE TEMPLE

When thoughts upon the wind have blown away
Like leaves of fall that tumble on the ground
Leaving but momentous themes to confound,
The pillars of the temples built dismay
Crowding darkling visions to mar each quest.

Then comes the funk of darkness mind must fight
Oppressed to find the answers written down
Have tainted laws for living that still drown
My thirst for answers with chains to indict
Seeking questions as error manifest.

I grieve I can't accept the temples built
With flawed pillars hewn from unworldly guilt.
10-25-94

BESIDE THE POND

A red winged blackbird is at hand
With *chirps* from limb nearby.
And now he trills
Throat warble thrills
Upon the air and sky.

Then just as quickly silence fills
View near dried reeds of pond
For he has flown
To place unknown
In search of mate beyond.

Yet swath of muskrat's swim is sown
In surge-lined brown head wake.
First such I've seen
This pond to wean
Through times my eyes partake.

But then is not the awe we glean
From out quaint nature lairs
A sought mist land
Mind growth expand
To comfort living cares?
4-13-01

LET US NOT SHOUT

Let us not shout
in crowded halls
of yesterday's vexation.

Waste not those tears
on beds of night
to pillars of fiery pain.

Make no badges
that glow in the heart
to dying delectation.

Carve ye no totems
plush cloaked for a shelf
extolling *past* romping in shame.

But shout to the skies
And cry with the heart
For paths you've yet to hew.

Make idols and lies
And kiss every tart
If it paints the future for you!
10-28-69

RIVER BANK SEDGE RE-GROWN TALL

Maple twirlers fill spring air,
Water soundings call,
White river flumes not seen but near
Through sheared bank sedge grown tall.

In morning with blue sky so clear
A favorite place is found
With river's waterfall not gone
Shade nook graced by its sound.

From planners plans, delayed, still drawn,
Relief is felt today,
Last year most thought falls would be lost
Till money woes held sway.

And though depression days have cost
Work, income, welfare care,
Here's river current is embossed
With beauty all may share.

And though we too have lost through wrongs
The river falls still sing sweet songs.
5-20-09

Treasure

KLINE CREEK FARM BRIDGE

Some yellow leaves float current's drift
Beneath wood bridge creek way,
A world apart of yesteryear
Quaint stopping place today
To view old farm house standing near
Past field of corn parched dry.

Farm lawn's defined by painted fence
White-green of cross board ply.

And gazing onto surface whence
The yellow leaves drift by
Below the rail on which I lean
More leaves twirl down from sky.

View paints old memory picture scene,
Found magic like leaf drift,
Of wending farm creek's rippling sheen
Which gave youth days a lift.

And here becomes new wonder place
To weave and conjure farm world grace.
10-08-05

THERE ARE WONDERS

I travel here, I travel there
I venture far and near
From river ponds to lake-sea coast
To meld with nature's sphere:

To grasp a signal from sky post,
To listen to the wind,
To watch the age old ritual's dance,
To mark and to rescind
The lies that would belief enhance
For private reasons bold,
To make compare and soothe mind's beast
In long entrenched stronghold
That came with birth and pleases least
When insight would be fair
At culling truth from knowledge feast
That's stored with blind eyed care.

And there are wonders that drift by
In nature's world beneath the sky!
6-15-01

EDENS FAR TO GLEAN

The golden threads among leaves green
Of willow by the pond
Seem roads entwined that lead to sky
With ocean stretched beyond!

Where waits strange worlds all drifting by:
White continent or isle,
Enchantment lands on view before
With echoes that beguile
As vapors twist and mountains soar,
Spawn lakes with linked delight,
Or bunch, with darkening shades of gray,
Gloom's density on white.

The willow's world where gold threads ray
Into blue astral scene
Is like our earth with dreams at play
Sought Edens far to glean!
6-27-04

PERFECT WAXEN YELLOW LEAF

I never know until work's done
What morning effort brings,
Till whisper's sigh
From out the sky
Injects some thought that sings?

Yet purpose says that I must try
To let ideas flow:
Sense, write, declare,
What's seen off there
In nature's morning glow.

And here this morning on the air
A yellow leaf is found,
Midst Summer's green
That fills the scene:
Etched image off the ground!

Brown table caught it fresh and clean,
Grace wonder, small to see:
Lost essence won
From tree undone
Brief life that tumbled free.

And now it rests upon my hand
Small, perfect, waxen leaf seen grand!
6-04-12

LOOKING, LOOKING INTO THE WELL

Looking, looking into the well
Of sky and land and sea
I seek to see what heart can tell
Of things that used to be

Is there some vibrant thread that's lost
Where value can be found
If only snatched from depths where tossed
From ages once profound

Some simple thing of quiet joy
That man has left behind
Forgotten in his quest to cloy
A thirst that won't unwind

There must be more that once was known
Before we got so smart
An inward peace that can be sown
While keeping pure in heart

And so I'm always looking deep
In wells that stretch before
To find a treasure I can keep
When joined to depth once more

6-28-95

HOW DIFFERENT ALL

How different all that's come to be
In life-years flight along.
No lasting fame,
No burnished name,
No eager fans that throng!

A common life, most days the same.
Our children prizes raised,
With children too,
Lives in review,
Who also must be praised!

The wonder family that we grew
Is wealth beyond compare:
A group of gold,
Spread talents bold
That now the world does share.

As parents who have now grown old
We look back with amaze,
And family see,
As it should be,
Love bound within our gaze!
8-09-13

Departure

ROBIN SIGHTING

A robin red breast's flashing wings
Flew into forest tree
As Summer wends
Leaf color blends
And fall about to be!

Yet robins come as Winter ends!
Spring's omen in our sky,
White snow around
Midst thawing ground
Bold sun's arch warmth on high.

And robins now should not be found
With us, as Summer strays.
Or so it's said
In paths I've tread
Throughout my living days.

But change within my life has bred
'Wind thoughts' not taught in school.
Where nature sings
Of many things
Lore's wisdom-sight can't rule.

As robin red breast near abides
Old lore with change once more collides!
9-14-09

LOTUS LADY

As morning sun wends passage way
Aslant above lake-sea
Upon still waters, vacant beach,
Lone figure form flows free.

Blonde woman on steel pier does reach
Svelte limbs in exercise.
Her legs, her arms stretch stanchion's band
Small surface for prone prize.

But not for gulls who watch at hand
On same perch out from shore
While lotus pose, at rest, she takes,
Still, Buddha like, before.

And in position sunlight makes
An aura lined display
Till past her form beach world awakes
With family come to play.

And then she's gone, fond memory sight,
Where once more lake-sea gave delight!
8-19-05

WHEN ROME ROARED AS A CHILD OF POWER

When Rome roared as a child of power
And Greece's glory glowed entire
There came on man one fateful hour
To cast aside his base desire
And choose a path that held a key
To spiritual doors of ecstasy

Then with new banner raised on high
And burning breasts of righteousness
The key was cast into the mire
While molding Rome to blessedness
The hour was gone, the key debased
As man his love of war embraced

1-28-70

Knot

ONE MORE RIVER

To wake one morning and find it's done
That it should end like this!
To have strained your back and mind and guts
Through hell's blackness toward light's bliss.

To dream sweet dreams of woman fair
In the sweat of your stink in the dark,
To smell perfume, the brush of her hair,
Then fight on with stench so stark.

And then to wake that mundane morn
Praying to death for his kiss,
Wishing to God you'd never been born
To find it had ended like this!

So here you are, alive but dead,
All meaning has turned where it fed:

No glory as dreamed
No elation's it's passed
You've won to the end that was schemed
Twas your foe who didn't last.

So now you're called to go back again
To return to the light and the bliss,
A past looming strange, bent, insane,
A meaningless artifice.

Then from the bowels of your soul you cry
Raging against these walls of time:
"Just one more river to cross, Oh God!
Just one more mountain to climb!"
4-21-1970

BATTLEFIELD

Wagon rolls with clatter drear
Wild blooms push out from death
The flies in heightened hum cohere
Foul ripeness gags each breath.
Heroes died and cowards turned
Where Glory's wrath was reaffirmed.

And all is memory, all is lost.

Jostling wagon rutty rolls
Through putrid field
's exhaust,
Through blood where clashed men's souls.

Darkened crime. Knelling time.

The bell beyond the meadow tolls
With pierce, persistent chime.

Now gather clouds to blot the sun
Rumbling thunder's discordant drum.
4-23-70
Published in Centres of Expression 2007
Publisher Noble House of London & New York

Mist

VIENNA MEMORY

The glowing of the lamp post
Shines on a midnight land
For raucous dins of daytime
Have faded in Time's sand.

And now the stilling hours
Which creep upon the scene
Bring forth those silent creatures
That daylight would demean.

The man with his wife's poodle,
The women on their beat,
The beggar who makes light of them,
The soldier down the street.

And over there, across the square,
The Opera has let out.
People stream, all furs and ties,
As taxis squeal about.

Soon lies the square deserted
Beneath a lamp lit night,
While falling snow in antic swirls
Paints midnight's world in white.
2-7-1969
Published in The International Library of Poetry 2007

JAMAICAN RECALL

It's like a tropic island scene
The beach, sea stretching blue,
Green trees that edge and flutter sky
Almost like date palm view.

The blue, the green, sand stretching by,
Bright water-colored scheme,
Evokes mind vision of far place
Jamaican in its theme.

There's only missing thatched hut grace
Which lined the once known beach
Recalling back those years ago,
Time picture rush from reach.

Familiar beach before does glow
With pastels rarely seen
Evoking mind trip vision show
As day's heat adds to scene.

While lake-sea readjusts for me
Past youthful time, evolves, floats free!
8-01-05

ECHOED WHISPERED PLAY

How many windows on the world
Are there impressing mind?
How much of focus leaves imprint
On memory cells to find?

I know today mind's picture print
Of lake and forest round
Will be confused and lost in space
With others from here found.

For often from this vantage place
I've watched the seasons change,
Watched Winter's snow and Springtime's birth
And Autumn's spectrum range.

Mind-memory blurs found treasured worth
Of shuffled lake-scene world
Like here today lawns greening earth
Beneath dark tree shapes furled,
But soon this window place will show
Leaves gracing hues through rich green's glow
And then what window shows today
Will be lost echo whisper play.
4-16-08

FLEET LIFE ON WINGS OF SONG

Although lake morning's sky is clear
—No clouds seen off away
—There is a mist that washes blue
With basking heat today.

I've chosen breezy oak hill view
As Summer drought around
Has curbed most echo pleasures known
Past *'wind thought*s*'* time had found.

But here, at least, the breezes sown
Make Summer come alive,
And lures the whispers from the sky
That urge me still to strive.

For as this year has wended by
Age pains have seeded fear
That out beyond rhyme words I ply
There's less and less to cheer!

It is, perhaps, time's space along
That fades fleet life on wings of song!
7-17-12

LOST ECHO RINGS

The names of plants and trees around
So common, lost to mind,
Which must be sought in reference book
Is wretched thought to find.

But true, so true, as now I look
On tree whose name I've known
And over there a blooming flower
That graces bed where sown.

And I deplore lost memory power
Of names I've not retained
Those common wonders often seen
Through years that I have gained.

And why does tree of leafy green,
Background to water's sound,
A common growth of river's scene
Have name that can't be found?

This is so true of many things
Of people, plants, lost echo rings!.
6-30-09

SENSED MOTION MYSTERY

Sometimes swift motion shape I see
From corner of my eye.
But when I turn it is not there!

Sensed motion here...blue sky!

And not just lakeside hill to share
Has shape seemed to abide;
But when at home, in mind work zone,
Gone something off to side!

And always when I've been alone,
At work projecting mind
Beyond life's daily habit things,
Poetic thought to find!

Perhaps mind fault illusion brings,
Sensed shape that cannot be,
From hidden world that often sings
Heard whispered sounds to me!

How strange to tell what I don't know.
And yet there is day's work to show!
9-19-07

BELL SONG MEMORY

White vapors drift upon sky's blue
With rain clouds off away
In Summer's dawn
June day has drawn
For morning's garden stay.

Before more rain high sun will spawn
Day's heat through June that flows,
Like past times known
Youth years long flown,
Fond image find that glows,

And now the bells at ten have sown
A music memory kept
Of Army times
In hotter climes
When heat had never slept.

For caissons echo in bell chimes
—*The Army's Marching Song*—
Camp Chaffee's view
Sweat trainee stew
Youth wondrous then and strong!
6-27-13

PETALUMA MORNING MIST

There's morning mist that filters trees
And blankets rolling hills
—So California picturesque—
Walled mesh that landscape fills.

Blurred picture hills seek image quest,
Emerging off away,
Although mist-grayness blends to sky
In morning passage play!

The lawn, the vineyard, stretched nearby
Are cleared of morning mist
As if enclosed, untouched and clear,
Unlike far landscape kissed.

Now overhead a faint blue smear
Seems layered high to tease
And makes cold's vapors disappear
For sunshine's heat to please.

Wild turkey flock vine's space invade
In show for me as far mists fade!
8-13-12

Connection

WIND WHISPERS SPUR

Pine needle lake shore shady place
In hot, hot humid day
With but faint breeze to cool caress
Is place of morning's stay.

For mind-sense urged: *'Grove won't oppress
As other places will!'*
Though on arrival, settling down,
Pines' atmosphere was still.

Then, like a greeting, wind force gown
Clothed coolness wrap on me,
As early whisper did infer
That here's where I should be.

And down the years wind whisper's spur
Has always offered grace,
Instilling thoughts, space-times that were,
When at said listening place.

For I'm an earth link to the sky
Through convoluting force on high!
7-11-08

LISTENING TO FALL'S WATER SOUND

I miss the lake-sea's roaring ways
Its winter ice mound shore;
I miss its quiet flat expanse
To sky curve seam before.

I miss its lapping waves in dance
That whispered *wind thoughts* free.
I miss and wonder if those times
Are but gone mystery?

Yet here found nature also limns
With lakes and river flows,
Its forest walks, here's waterfall,
The times past-farm-world sows.

All these and Arboretum's call
Replace far lake-sea ways!
But will new wonders grow or pall
In future's wending days?

So far there's comfort in what's found
While listening to fall's water sound.

7-13-06

DANADA NATURE

I took a nature walk today
On trail most new to me
Off from horse farm, so picturesque,
That I had come to see.

And on the trail a squirrel at rest
Reared up with stately pose
In search around for noise he heard,
Twitch turning head and nose.

He spotted me as chattering bird
Had given him alarm.
Or so I thought, though all around
Bird notes filled air with charm.

Squirrel scampered off to higher ground
But paused, with reared display,
To pose again like statue found
Ere going on his way!
5-22-06

POETRY IN THE SKY

There's poetry up in the sky
Where soars black raptor wings,
Turn gliding, stretched, upon the air,
Float motion circling rings.

I stop and gaze, ten minutes there!
Like glider plane by shore,
Bird rides wind thermals high aloft,
Flight grace inscribed before.

And then, at length, wings break stretch, soft,
Change angled flight sky's way,
To soar fresh course through background blue
With wings slight two-flap flay!

But then its gone, slow glide review,
Of hawk or eagle high,
Black feathered grace flight soar to view,
Enchantment in the sky!
5-09-07

COYOTES

First mother came and then her young,
Coyotes from near wild,
To eat red fruits dropped from lawn's tree
Which squirrels also beguiled.

Such lovely creatures roaming free
Tan fur marked health glow signs,
Well fed and hearty nosing lawn
Fox face-like gracing lines.

They came again with snow withdrawn;
The young one skittish tame
Like hunting dog with speed shape fair
In dash pursuit of game.

With sadness-joy I'd watch them there,
Wild vicious creatures sung,
Partaking of dropped red fruit fare
Lawn's Christmas tree had flung.

They've not returned for quite awhile
Yet memory's image brings a smile.
2-17-09

THE AURA PRESENT

The feeling extraordinarily rare
Compares not with the taste of vintage wine
Yet of note when tempted to define
The aura present when I know you're there
And feel your laughter caressing, "Hello."

Our thoughts mix conversational comment
'Til I know self wedded common to thee
Yet wonder where you roam when far from me
Elated by your views so impudent
Yet so refreshing strange as they bestow.

You've changed me for the better I avow
Aware that when you're gone you're here somehow.
9-15-94

PRAYER

Let faith restore my soul again
With strength more like the sea
And though on surface turmoils howl,
Winds whipping rage so free,
May quietness at heart remain
Which storms cannot befoul.

Let humor fill impatient ways
With warmth more like the sun,
A blazing chariot through days
Where laughter's course does run.

Let love ferment each family tie
To bloom like earth each spring
And flood the air with thriving peace
Wherein cold hearts will sing.

In God's design let me beautify
Each work with simple grace
That all who see may testify:
"He revered his Father's face."
4-14-70

DUCK WITH ROYAL TIARA

A lovely park with old shade trees
Sonoma Center Square
So many ducks, brown, black and white
Upon small duck pond there.

A small bridge in sun's filtered light
Divides quaint pond split view
With lush reed stand at bushy end
Near white fan grass high spew.

So picturesque, pond water's wend
A feeding trough splash mall
And duck with seeming powder puff
Stands out amongst them all.

Light tan surrounds its head's cream fluff,
A royal crown grown tease.
Duck sails alone then poses ruff
Grace profile there to please.

I snap royal portrait, reed lines by,
As duck flicks tail but does not fly.
10-01-01

Construct

A BOTTLE HAS INTRINSIC WORTH

Intriguing are the shapes of things
That fill our daily lives
To ease the load of life on earth
Beyond instinctual drives.

A bottle has intrinsic worth
Containing liquids used;
Yet some of elegant design
Hold fantasies infused:
With flutes and stoppered glass entwined,
Hued ornaments to grace
A shelf or nook for mind world weave
No liquids to embrace.

This proves man's godhead I believe
From other living things!
For we mold earth and can perceive
What art with being brings.
8-02-06

LAGOON RENAMED 'BASIN LAKE'

What is the essence words can give?
What mental pictures make?
The garden people now have changed,
—With sign— *lagoon* to *'Lake!'*

But yet flow twisting waters ranged
Below park's boundary lines
Are called *lagoons*, just as before,
Old status which defines!

And is here really changed at core?
Despite vast monies spent?
Like *nouveau riche* in costly dress
What has such new name lent?

Is there some noble consciousness
In what a name will give?
Words glossing *past* with bright success
As pride drives how we live?

6-22-04

MIND IMAGE NAME

'*Star Mist*' seems recalled flowers' name!
In walking past bloom flow,
Where no sign marks white petals fair,
Long lasting garden show.

My mind with daisies does compare
What's tantalized so long,
White petals low, starred scarlet core,
Low wonder morning's song!

And as I gazed on them once more,
Where garden worker hoed,
He phoned and asked and then told me
With gaze on blooms that flowed.

They're *Zinnias,* so fresh to see,
With '*Star Mist*' not their name!
Forgetful hearing, lost words flee,
Impressions mind grope game.

Then beauty's image seemed to say:
'*Star Mist! is my name for today!*'
9-11-13

MONOLITHS

We think in terms of monoliths:
The night, the foe, the country, man,
Till masses mighty grow stern myths
Beyond sane reach within our span.
Fresh thoughts to think inspire such fear
That sordid meanness is held dear.

"The world is round!" Columbus said.
Remember all the fear that fed?

So insignificant we seem
In thought of self against the whole
We damn the whole for selfish dream
And let mad ego seize control:
*"Let all the world at my feet fall
For I am great and you are small!"*

Worlds make worlds as our mind bestows
The grain in which a monolith grows.
4-27-70

Seasons

BIRD VOICES HEARD TODAY

There are bird voices heard today
—Unlike love songs of Spring—
In flight response to hunger cries
The dawns of Summer bring.

Yet here, already, Summer flies,
Gone June so cool and damp,
More rain last month than normal seen
Extending Spring world's stamp.

But now true Summer grips the scene,
Lush grass lawns green now streaked
With blades of brown, bloom clover white
Through lushness that has peaked!

And while cool days still bring delight,
With scorching heat allay,
The birds seen darting round in flight
Are in a family way.

The trilling of love's Spring-float song
Replaced by chirps from nests along.
7-07-09

WEATHER'S CHANGING FACE

The leaves are rustling overhead
The breeze is cool force flow
The night was chill into the dawn
Sky here is cloud free show.

The Autumn seasoned morning's spawn
Is not too different strange
Although official Summer days
Have not yet spent their range.

For every year within my gaze,
Reporting consciously,
I've noted weather season's swings
Outside of normalcy!

I'm happiest when Summer sings
And saddest when it's fed
With raging floods and horrid things
Experienced instead!

Yet life in time should make one think:
What's good? What's bad? From which to drink?
9-13-13

LITTLE MEN

Pitter, pitter, patter, pit,
On the mushroom stools we sit
Little men you cannot see
Scoring nature's symphony

Leaves of yellow, leaves of brown
Twirling up and falling down
Winter's coming, summer's done
Autumn's colors now are spun

Red and yellow hues we taint
On the trees with magic paint
Here we stir and mix and play
Till our work is swept away

Boys and girls with happy faces
Dashing through our leafy traces
Make our work a jolly one
Ere the winter winds have come

10-29-69

Cantigny

Cantigny Park is a publicly accessible 500-acre park in Wheaton, Illinois. It was a donation made from the former estate of Joseph Medill and his grandson Colonel Robert R. McCormick, who were non-consecutively editor/publishers of the Chicago Tribune newspaper between 1860 and 1927. Cantigny is beautifully set in its Suburban Chicago locale and includes large formal and informal gardens, two museums, a 27-hole golf course, a picnic grove, a playground, hiking paths, restaurants and a gift shop. The poet has spent many pleasurable hours in the Cantigny Park and it has inspired much poetry some of which is included in the following section. The park gets its name from the World War I battle in which American troops first became significantly involved in 1917. Robert McCormick was a participant in the battle as an officer in the artillery. As a commemoration, McCormick acquired some surplus military equipment including some tanks that are displayed in Cantigny park and are a part of its unique identification.

CANTIGNY POND

The pond with fountain grips my sight
Upon Cantigny walk,
Bells tolling hour from tower near,
Air filled with children talk.

But they move on and water's sphere,
White sprayed foam spill on high,
Has splashing circle splatter sounds
As bell tones cease nearby.

A cardinal's song from tree expounds
To blend with fountain's voice
In morning place I've come today
Where each sound does rejoice.

But soon I'll wander on my way
With beauty left and right,
Blown crab trees flowered on the day
To feed roam-strolling sight.

Cantigny bursts each view with grace
My wondrous new found writing place!
Wind chimes pick up bells tolling throng
With notes to echo tower's song.

4-21-10

EXEDRA

I spelled it wrong, and knew not sense it made,
—On pictured image taken of this scene—
Where now I sit surrounded by lush green
And tall oak trees, aside, whose branches shade
Out sky above EXEDRA's walk to tomb.

I used an *'H'* for sound heard in my mind,
Away from place of pictured flower bowl,
Where leaves of red, with herbage round the whole
Of granite's white, have molded dogs reclined
Below a central cross adorning tomb.

Monuments's half circle wall of white rings
Has end-bench side with sculpted eagle wings!
And here *'McCormick'* of Cantigny lies
Amidst groomed beauty's scene and symbol's guise.
8-18-10

WHITE 'HEDRA' TOMB

As now I know I'd best explain
Before thought blurs it all:
'An ancient conversation room'
EXEDRA does enthrall.

And yet side wings of sculpted plume,
Dogs in Egyptian style,
The Christian Cross of giant seat,
Confuses sense awhile!

As *'hedra'* is Greek word for 'seat'
Thought *'h'* was not that wrong.
And plaque I found and read today
Defines white granite's song.

For here is granite's grand display,
Which nature should not stain,
As granite came from far away
Whose white hue does remain.

Memorial should long abide
Though few converse here on time's tide.
8-19-10

CANTIGNY'S CARILLON

I wait this morning for a song
The Carillon may play.
For ten of morning's not yet passed
When clock tolls time of day.

Five minutes do the bell tones last
For I clocked song last time.
And now I wonder if songs change
When bells are set to chime?

And I must be just here, in range,
When sounds will ring bells cheer!
For yesterday, clock's toll through space,
Drift floated faint to hear.

The bells now ring atonal lace
Of music sounds along
Much other than first time's heard grace
Which played a well known song.

So now I've learned bells keyed remote
Are menu changed each day songs float!
8-20-10

FIVE BUCKEYES

I haven't had a buckeye walk
For years and years and years.

But there on lawn Cantigny's way,
—As mid September nears—
Some ripened buckeyes brightened day
Cracked open on the grass!

And so I stopped and gathered five
Beneath tree's laden mass.

Green hanging spheres on limbs still thrive,
With sharpened spikes on rind.
So different from Vienna trees
Of buckeyes there we'd find.

As olden memory thoughts did please,
—*Midst daughter's child voice talk*—
I stooped and found five nuts to seize
Ere ambling on with walk.

These shiny brown nuts home I'll place
For table decoration's grace!
9-08-10

CANTIGNY 'SCHOOL DAYS'

It's 'School Days' here upon lawn's way
—White tents, small, pegged around—
With Revolutionaries seen
In garb those days propound!

School children gather by tent scene
—With two brass cannon near—
Spread table there with tales told
Of new born nation's fear.

Brass artifacts, like burnished gold,
Fill table's cloth arrayed
With kitchen housewares that age used
—Tent close to wood fire laid.

And for a moment, time abused,
—George Washington strode day—
Past me and white tents where I mused
On Age long passed away!
9-09-10

THREE HALLOWEEN FIGURES

Too soon, I think, and yet I see
In garden walk along
Three figures stuffed for Halloween
Midst flowers Summer song!

Haystacks and pumpkins not yet seen
Although each year they're found
To grace October's garden pall
With spooks and ghouls around.

I wonder why? These three on call?
Before the Summer's done
Although their figures add quaint spice
Of Autumn's trick-treat fun.

This startling sight I still find nice
Midst flowers flowing sea
An early Halloween sphere slice
Of Autumn's color spree.

Too early yet but still reminds
Brown buckeyes now are treasured finds!
9-18-13

CANTIGNY'S EDEN MOLD

Lush green and lovely every place
I've strolled through garden ways,
With rain and sun
Through season spun,
Year's antic weather plays.

With all the ups and downs begun,
Tornadoes, fires and flood,
Cantigny here,
Bloom flower sphere,
Still has its relic blood.

The tanks, museum's atmosphere,
However of time's past,
Still lets park bind
With far world's kind
Of tragedies now cast.

Yet beauty that is here to find,
Each peaceful garden found,
Where colors race
Blooms artful grace
Now seems like sacred ground.

And I am blessed each time I'm here
In gardens well groomed atmosphere!
6-14-13

BUCKEYE TREE'S SHADED BENCH

Engulfed by shade of buckeye tree
On bench I've found today
Is morning's place with noisy leaves
Breeze force flow's rattling play.

Leaf sounds are not from buckeye trees
But others edging walk
Where leaves are small and twirl around
Which makes them seem to talk.

The buckeye leaves are more profound
Large shapes that sway force flow
And show spiked green cling buckeye balls
That Summer seasons grow.

It's Autumn when each buckeye falls
Brown nuts on ground to see
Which always foreign way recalls
With times that used to be.

These buckeye trees seem old and wise
With shaded bench day gift surprise!
7-24-13

SEASON'S COLORS CAUGHT

Amazing days Cantigny's way
Mums' colored spectrum place
Though trees around don't share bright hues
Of Autumn's season grace.

Tree crowns are green or wilting views
Of curling brown cling shades
With hints of yellow-orange found
In off-walk distant glades.

Yet mums and other flowers round
Let Autumn come alive,
Uplifting gardens that delight
Where spectrum colors thrive.

And also cheerful season sight
Each Halloween array
Stuffed figures and Fall pumpkins bright
Throughout each garden way.

Cantigny's world of color gleams
With straw stuffed figures to haunt dreams!
10-09-13

THE 4TH HAS MORNING SUN

I've sought a quiet garden place,
Secluded nature's way,
Off from all celebration's din
This Independence Day!

This bench I've found, beside, within,
Cantigny's pathway maze
Is near yet off from bells that toll
Day's song of time's felt praise!

The morning's free of clouds dark scroll
That's washed mid-west with rain
And lets sun's heat reverberate
Away from gloom's bleak stain.

This spawning sun may now create
Sought Summer's span of grace
Denied by weather woes of late
But warming now this place!

Now off away the crowds around
Make joyous holiday voiced sound!
7-04-13

NO WISE THOUGHT TO SHARE

The thoughts that come and drift away
Are nowhere near profound.
Just catalogue of what I see
In morning's garden round.

Red blooms and white, green speckled tree,
—Midst group of different hues—
Crown green with shadow-etched sunlight,
Enhancing flower views.

And though I grope for thought insight,
Immortal words to fly
Eternal wonder of delight
Forever 'neath earth's sky,
There's only garden's beauty here
In flowers perfumed atmosphere!

Yet someday soon, not far away,
I trust wise thought will come to play!
8-09-13

CANTIGNY WONDERS STRANGE

My first full wander walking day
Cantigny gardens wealth display
With every garden plot unchanged
Midst sense impressions impact strange!

For all is other while the same
In time's ongoing space-flow game:
The trees, the flowers blooming near
Evoking morning's mythic cheer.
Yet different qualities flow free
From essences that used to be!

While spectrum colors still abound
—Groom workers spraying water round—
The Carillon which now tolls ten
Holds silent echoes unlike when
I came for morning music played
Midst wealth and grandeur's world arrayed!
And while all's lush like times before
Bells ring out no ten music score!

Of course I know that I'll return
For essences yet to discern!
6-16-14

Art

FOR THOSE WHO WOULD WISH TO KNOW

For those who would wish to know, let me say
The rushing waters with their cleansing taste
Don't often wash with diamonds interlaced
But flood streambed with flotsam gone astray
Carried from the mountain passes by storm.

Debris' shards must be borne to cull the stone
So prized for rarity and flashing light
From facets depth winking an inner sight
Startling the mind with passion to enthrone
And cull again for riches to inform.

The miner with constancy washes all
Or finds another stream which can enthrall.

6-07-94

CHARMAIN LONDON'S 'HOUSE OF HAPPY WALLS'

The up-slant forest hill path here,
—Jack London's State Park place—
Has bench where I've paused now to sit
By *'Happy Walls'* stoned face!

The Wolf House Ruins are down a bit,
On winding mountain track.
And while I thought of going there
Leg pains have held me back.

The *'House of Happy Walls,'* stone fare,
On mountain's top by me,
Contains, compressed, Jack's history told,
Walls filled by lives lived free!

It's all and more, two lives bound bold,
With model *'Snark'* displayed.
There, listed too, all books Jack sold
That held rapt world engaged.

Beside stone house, tree log on hill
Sleeps rattler: source of shrieks or thrill!
8-13-12 (Glen Ellen, CA.)

ALA FITZGERALD

Oft times I re-read others verse
That's long infected me
With awe and wisdom that impressed
Word magic's majesty!
Then when *'Wind Thoughts'* were first expressed
With rhyme forms crafted new
To hold day's thought
Fleet time had sought
I often felt such view
Could also fit within forms wrought
Which genius of old had caught!

Infectious rhyme scheme fills my mind
Fitzgerald verses there to find
Translating Khayyam's thought and sense
Exploding fame worldwide and hence!
And so this morning I will try
To be like Edward as thoughts fly:

If I should learn what evermore would be
Would I exploit for self its mystery?
Or keep it secret, hidden through my time,
Rejoicing without name when I'm set free?

Or would I shout to worldly skies the news
And reap wine's golden harvest with such views,
A cornucopia through pleasure's game
Until the scythe of wonder body hews?

And yet I know, and know not, what is said
As life determines footsteps days have bred
And while the dawning sun pales starry night
I greet the morning pathways still ahead!

Those sentiments have filtered with the dawn
Expressed in way Fitzgerald might have drawn.

But now I set my pen aside
Content with morning's *'wind thought'* ride!

8-30-07
This was published in 'The BEST of 2007 Poems and Poets" by the International Library of Poetry

INDEX

#
1890 Farm's Appeal, *Road and Return*, 52
1890'S Historic Farm Contrast, *Vantage*, 22

A
A Bottle Has Intrinsic Worth, *Construct*, 88
Ala Fitzgerald, *Art*, 111
A Little While, *Symphony*, 9
Ancient Chinese Wilderness Poetry, *Pull*, 33
And Do I Really Care?, *Vantage*, 21
And Would You Lead Another Life?, *Seed*, 3
Angel Haired Goddess, *Seed*, 4
Art, 109

B
Battlefield, *Knot*, 71
Bell Song Memory, *Mist*, 78
Beside The Pond, *Release*, 58
Bird Chorus Morning, *Symphony*, 8
Bird Voices Heard Today, *Seasons*, 92
Blue Dragonfly, *Play*, 14
Brown Oak Leaf Cling, *Release*, 54

Buckeye Tree's Shaded Bench, *Cantigny*, 104

C
Camelot's Dream, *Vantage*, 15
Cantigny, 95
Cantigny Pond, *Cantigny*, 96
Cantigny 'School Days', *Cantigny*, 102
Cantigny Wonders Strange, *Cantigny*, 108
Cantigny's Carillon, *Cantigny*, 99
Cantigny's Eden Mold, *Cantigny*, 103
Change And Recall, *Road and Return*, 46
Charmain London's 'House of Happy Walls', *Art*, 110
Come! Walk with Me , *Road and Return*, 49
Connection, 80
Consider, *Play*, 11
Construct, 88
Coyotes, *Connection*, 84

D
Danada Nature, *Connection*, 82
Days of Summer Wander On, *Pull*, 28
Day's Song, *Symphony*, 6

Departure, 67
   Distortion's Gaze, *Veil*, 43
   Dream Fantasy, *Veil*, 41
   Duck with Royal Tiara, *Connection*, 87

E
Echoed Whispered Play, *Mist*, 74
Edens Far To Glean, *Treasure*, 63
Exedra, *Cantigny*, 97

F
Fish Splash Lure, *Pull*, 31
Five Buckeyes, *Cantigny*, 100
Fleet Life on Wings of Song, *Mist*, 75
For Those Who Would Wish To Know, *Art*, 109
Fresh Perspectives, *Vantage*, 23

H
How Different All, *Treasure*, 66
Huge Boulder Rock, *Pull*, 32

I
In Time Space Wend Along, *Seed*, 2
In the Woods with Far Desire, *Veil*, 36

J
Jamaican Recall, *Mist*, 73

K
Kline Creek Farm Bridge, *Treasure*, 61
Kline Creek Farm Scene, *Road and Return*, 47
Knot, 70

L
Lagoon Renamed 'Basin Lake', *Construct*, 89
Lake-Sea and Ocean's Grace, *Road and Return*, 51
Lake-Sea's Unseen Face, *Vantage*, 18
Let Us Not Shout, *Release*, 59
Listening To Fall's Water Sound, *Connection*, 81
Little Men, *Seasons*, 94
Lone Gull Home, *Road and Return*, 48
Looking, Looking Into the Well, *Treasure*, 65
Lost Echo Rings, *Mist*, 76
Lotus Lady, *Departure*, 68

M
Measured Time, *Release*, 53
Mind Image Name, *Construct*, 90

Mind View Force, *Veil*, 34
Mist, 72
    Monoliths, *Construct*, 91
    Morning Shadows Creep,
        Symphony, 7
    Mother Nature's Morning
        Tease, *Pull*, 30

N
    No Wise Thought To Share,
        Cantigny, 107

O
    One More River, *Knot*, 70

P
    Petaluma Morning Mist, *Mist*,
        79
    Perfection Striving, *Vantage*,
        19
    Perfect Waxen Yellow Leaf,
        Treasure, 64
    Perspective Truth, *Vantage*, 20
    Pillars of the Temple, *Release*,
        57
Play, 11
    Poetry in the Sky, *Connection*,
        83
    Prayer, *Connection*, 86
Pull, 27

R
    Red Maple Leaves, *Veil*, 39
Release, 53
    River Bank Sedge Re-Grown
        Tall, *Release*, 60
    River Bend's Autumn Scene,
        Vantage, 17
Road and Return, 46
    Robin Sighting, *Departure*, 67

S
    Sandpiper, *Play*, 12
Seasons, 92
    Season's Colors Caught,
        Cantigny, 105
Seed, 1
    Sensed Motion Mystery, *Mist*,
        77
    Sky's Ocean Shore, *Symphony*,
        10
    Sonoma's Portuguese Beach
        with Gull, *Vantage*, 26
    Soul's Worth Goal, *Pull*, 29
    Sound Mysteries Sought, *Veil*,
        38
Symphony, 6

T
    The 4th Has Morning Sun,
        Cantigny, 106
    The Bark, *Veil*, 45

The Books are too Many, *Veil*, 40
The Other Side of Yesterday, *Road and Return*, 50
There are Wonders, *Treasure*, 62
The Aura Present, *Connection*, 85
The Sea Gulls, *Release*, 56
The Wayward Heart, *Pull*, 27
Thought Passage Vital Force, *Seed*, 1
Three Halloween Figures, *Cantigny*, 102
Treasure, 61
Two Poplar Seeds, *Seed*, 5

V

Van Gogh's Astound, *Vantage*, 25
Vantage, 15
Veil, 34
Vienna Memory, *Mist*, 72

W

Weather's Changing Face, *Seasons*, 93
What Eyes Allow, *Veil*, 37
What, Into the Nightingale's Song, *Veil*, 35
What Is True Knowledge?, *Veil*, 42
When Into Darkness, *Release*, 55
When Rome Roared as a Child of Power, *Departure*, 69
When Rome Roared as a Child of Power, *Veil*, 44
White *'Hedra'* Tomb, *Cantigny*, 98
Wind Whispers Spur, *Connection*, 80
Wonder's Spell, *Vantage*, 16

Z

Zen Garden (*Kare-San-Sui*), *Vantage*, 24

www.ingramcontent.com/pod-product-compliance
Lightning Source LLC
LaVergne TN
LVHW011425080426
835512LV00005B/271